THE WOODCARVER'S WIFE

The Woodcarver's Wife

poems by

Sherry Chandler

WIND PUBLICATIONS

Copyright © 2014 by Sherry Chandler. Printed in the United States of America. All rights reserved. No part of this book may be reproduced in any manner, except for brief quotations embodied in critical articles or reviews. For information, address Wind Publicatiions, 600 Overbrook Drive, Nicholasville, Kentucky 40356.

International Standard Book Number 978-1-936138-66-1
Library of Congress Control Number 2013956830

First edition

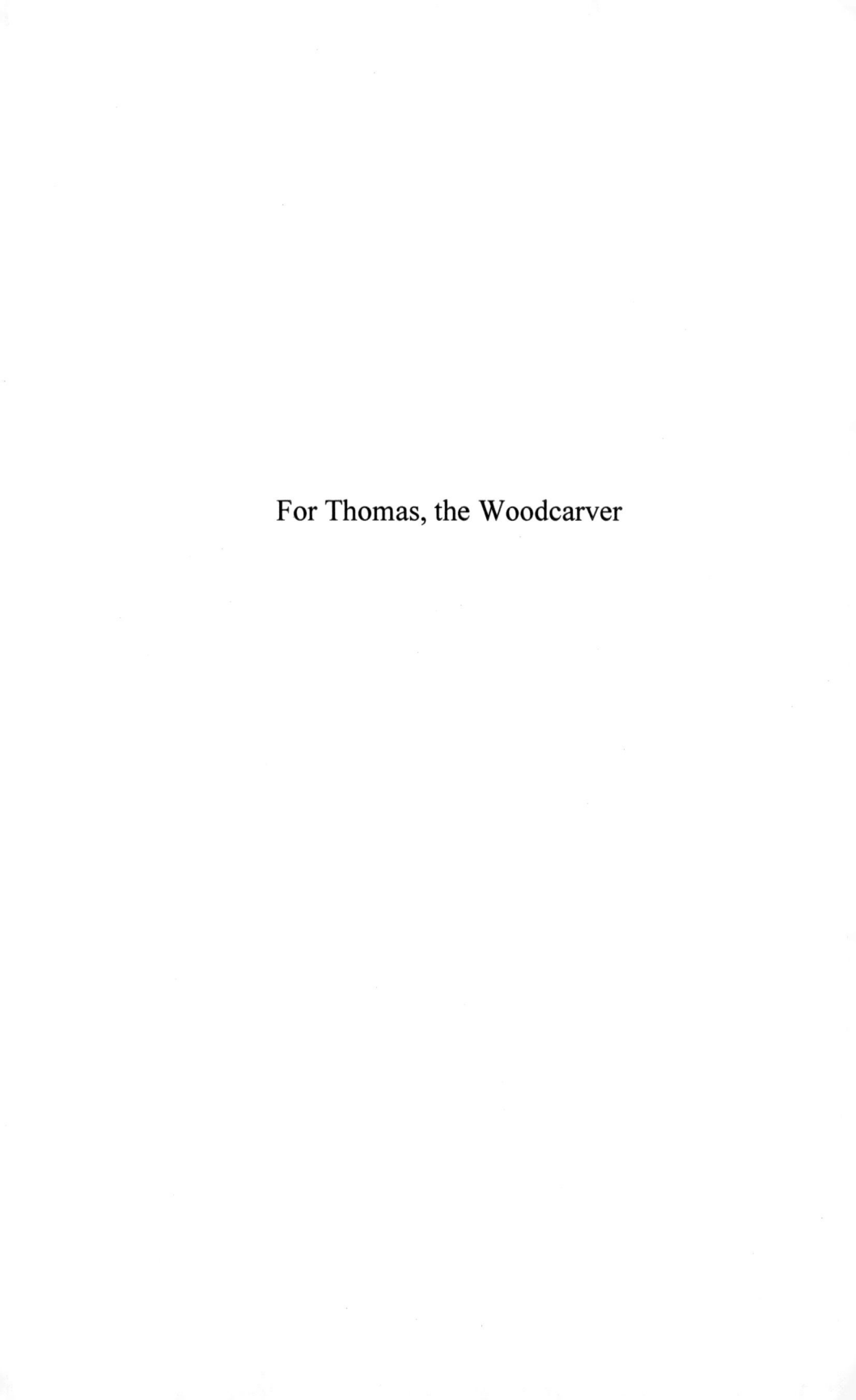

For Thomas, the Woodcarver

Contents

I

Amateur Photography	1
Talking Graduate School Blues	2
Meek	3
We Pledged to Hold Together Like Sisters	4
Sonnenizio On a Line From Hayden Carruth	6
Bennet's *New Latin Grammar* (1895): A Love Poem	7
Against Panache	8
Clearing Out	9
Looking West	10
An Accounting	11
Atmospheric Conditions	12
Rough Winds	13
Feeding the Birds	14
For My Valentine, a Modern Pastural With a Lot of Bull	15
Ephemera	16
Homeplace with Birds and Trees	17
Jaws of Life	18
Bonfire	20
Residency	21
An Old Lover's Invitation to Practice a Different Alchemy	22

II

The Woodcarver's Wife	25

III

Fulcrum	33
On the Eve of Leap Day	34
First Day of Spring	35
Playing Chicken	36
Poem Beginning With a Line From Helen Losse	37
Memento Mori	38
Pantoum for Late Spring	39

Pterophylla camellifolia	40
Garlic	41
Toxicodendron radicans	42
Hummingbirds	43
Tobacco Barn	44
August Tomatoes	46
End of Summer	47

IV

Doxology	51
Duet	52
After 40 Years	53
Hearth Goddess	54
Clothes Make the Man	55
What Bugs Us	56
Attrition	57
Wasted	58
Dissonance	59
Diagnosis	60
A Fairytale	61
Aubade	62
Medjool Dates	63
Dry October	64
Numerology	65
Stitches Out of Time	66
Christmas Day, 2010	67
Saturday Morning Cartoons	68
Beginning	70
Acknowledgements	73

I

Amateur Photography

For Thomas on His 61st Birthday

I took this snap in seventy-seven,
stopped you with lips shaped
to your breath, flames bowing but no

wish granted. You sit, hands clasped,
prim in the fake cable sweater I crocheted.
By chance the Polaroid distilled,

curving from that acrylic cuff,
the slender grace of your wrist,
an art beyond my skill.

I was after the burning candles,
the wish breath bent, didn't know
that photos capture loss.

I want to tease that wrist with my finger
the way a child might trace
the letters of her name.

I'd learn a hunger for more than cake,
a flame that consumes
and with each consummation fires again.

Talking Graduate School Blues

The practicable epic of the history of English ideas —
my journal says you yelled it while you slept
one June morning thirty-five years ago.
What were the graduate school sirens, what the storms
on bookish seas that swept you onto the shoals
of such a sprung rhythm? On that same night
I burrowed into an underworld revealed
in Granny's root cellar. I wrote it down —
same old tunnel, same old spiders in the crannies —
still hoping for some sign I was a star
too brilliant for the given role — supporting bit
as wife of the gifted. That was before I learned
that even the clever can't dig their way free.
You lectured in your sleep, I fought off orb
weavers — hundreds dropped from webs I tore,
dream-driven to explore the passageway
I'd found behind Ball jars of peaches and beans.

Meek

Eve with sad demeanor meek
       — John Milton

The word squeaks like a cornered mouse. Be it
Eve or Mary, meek and mild means man
on top. Why not a girlchild wild, unyielding?
No weak sister, she, a girl who'd ride
astride. What worth do we assign Christ's promise
for the meek? Is that inheritance a six-foot plot
in which to rot and to earth return?
Inferior, who is free? asked Milton's Eve.
She bit, and in the biting forged the chains
enslaving all her unborn daughters to the *God
in him*. The fall gal takes the rap.
What twice-blind manner of man creates and then
destroys a woman who can ask that question?

We Pledged to Hold Together Like Sisters

When she was in the room I watched her
like a field mouse watches an orange cat.

Her double-jointed fingers, holding
a Marlboro long, curved backwards,
as though they had no bones.

Her Iranian husband — *Persian*, he said —
invoked Cyrus and Darius, a civilization
old when Britons painted themselves blue.

Her skirts too short, tops too tight
for the weight she carried, I judged her cheap,
until one day we were fast friends.

Her hair brassy, her skin too pale,
her eyes too bright a green, she laughed
too loud, showed too much gum.

Her Persian husband boasted of a poet
father, adolescent scrapes, narrow
escapes from the Shahanshah's secret police.

The summer I stayed in her upstairs room,
the summer I married in her front parlor,
the summer Abolfazl spent in Tehran,

I heard the phantom footsteps. The click
of heel on wood came down the hall
and stopped, didn't climb the stairs,

the summer I couldn't understand
why his going frightened her,
the summer her house was haunted.

Sonnenizio On a Line From Hayden Carruth

The fury of romance, surging, resurging, wet —
that was not our way — well, maybe wet —
but not the storm surf's crashing wet.
Ours was rain after drought, a wet
that heals cracked earth. Or that car-window wet —
a muggy night on lover's lane — the wet
of captured breath, the swollen wet
of skin on skin, the splashing wet
juices of youth. I have witnessed the wet
red blood of fury, seen the wailing wet
tidal salt of sobs that thrashed wet
rocks to sand. I need no shattering wet
for we have sparkled wet as sun on dry
champagne, danced wet as an April sky.

Bennet's *New Latin Grammar* (1895): A Love Poem

tecum ludere sicut ipsa possem
et tristis animi levare curas
 — Gaius Valerius Catullus

Though your cover is frayed at the edges, gold
lettering dimmed, the upper left-hand corner
defaced along the spine by water-stains,
slip stitches hold your binding tight.
The years that yellowed your pages could not degrade
your charts (*accusative of the result produced*)
and lists (*subjunctive by attraction*). I try
to learn by heart your conjugations (*moods*
of indirect discourse), mutter third declension
into my pillow at 3:00 a.m. (*dative*
of person judging). Skittish as an overbred mare,
memory refuses to stand for copulatives
and supines, balks at figures of rhetoric, stumbles
on dactylic foot and caesura. Diastole, systole,
intricate rhythms elude, conventions of the ablative
erode. Parataxis, hypotaxis, clauses of wish
and proviso run through my brain like water
through a sieve and anyway I'm sleepy.
You'll never be a page-turner, but I've devoted
years to probing the subtleties of your extensive index.

Against Panache

My love is not Roxanne's for Cyrano,
a single rose lost in hothouse words,
nor is my love like Cyrano's absurd
obsession, blinded by his outsized nose,

his outsized wit, his sharp priapic sword.
It isn't Christiàn's — comely but dumb —
no willing dupe for Cyrano's aplomb,
no speechless slave to Cyrano's word horde.

You'll find my love a homelier affair,
less enticed by style — the plume, the pen —
than by the plow. The slow thrust of its blade
isn't *savoir faire* but table fare.
My love is grounded, my love does not pretend,
it feeds on bread, not strutting gasconade.

Clearing Out

Who knows what will document a life?

Who decides whether to keep the clippings
from *Progressive Farmer*, instructions
for running farm machines long sold
scrawled on the backs of window envelopes,
years of Christmas letters neatly packaged?

Your passivity wore out my patience so I stripped
the sheets from the bed she died on, turned the mattress,
bagged up syringes and plastic tubes, tossed the stacks
of carefully washed cottage-cheese cartons.

She took sick in August, died in November.
I worked all through January in the cold house,
trying to separate treasure from trash.

Some things were easy — no one could wear
the size 5 Girl Scout shoes, the crepe dress from
Marshall Field 1942, red, chic, swathed in plastic.

Some things I discovered and rediscovered —
tortured shapes of tree fungus, a pilfered chunk
of the petrified forest, a dusty starfish,
one leg broken off at the tip, a bracelet, each
link the flag of an Allied Nation.

Looking West

Sometimes a freight train crawls
along our afternoon, small
as a toy, its ends obscured by trees.
More often it rumbles through our sleep.
If the weather's right,
it rattles the windows.
The two-lane blacktop makes
a nearer line, the western edge
of what we claim as ours,
embanked in irises and lilies.
Between, a wide expanse
where morning mists rise
sometimes on corn,
sometimes on grass,
where the westering sun lays
its long shadows.
Though the field belongs to our neighbor,
and we've set no foot upon it
these thirty years,
we are more intimate than he
with the late night rumble of CSX freight,
the song of the meadowlark
that stands guard on its nest
from the fencerow,
the ways light dawns and dies
as the metronome sun
swings north and south.

An Accounting

>after Elizabeth Barrett Browning

I have no need to count those well-known ways
when owls are singing in the hour before daylight
and I must pause and listen as one might
to a still small voice. For me you are one graced

by those great horned owls, the spirits of this place,
the steady hand you offer when the flight
is steep, the way you court the fretboard to invite
the tune, from blues shuffle to minor ballad phrase.

The owls begin their pair-calling duet
under the Hunger Moon, their fluting breath
the year's first hymn to light and life renewed.
Their harmonies sound the tonic across the breadth
of our farm — I am here. Where are you? —
till the waxing Sap relieves the Hunger's depths.

Atmospheric Conditions

        with apologies to Johnny Mercer

We shall have weather
whether we want it or not. Days
may be cloudy or sunny, as some clever
writer has said. On the whole
I'd say we'd rather
have the sun for if it rains
we shall get wetter,
and if the day is wuthering,
our umbrellas will invert
making us madder
than a wet hen. But then
if we have too much noonday sun
we'll be up to our withers
in hydrophobic dogs and Englishmen.

Though I can claim neither
my hair nor my sins
have been washed whiter
than snow, I'm sad to say
I have not weathered
all that well. Though I'm too
well-nourished to claim I've withered
on the vine, my hopes for a hale
old age have blown away
I know not whither.
I guess I sheepishly followed the knell
of the wrong bellwether.

But as we huddle in the cellar
sheltering from life's norwester
I only hope we will not waver.

Rough Winds

after Shakespeare's Sonnet 18

When, at the end of a long and tedious day,
I blow my cool and have a temper fit
and you retreat in anger and dismay
to brood among your scorps and router bits,

when I have scrubbed and buffed until floors shine,
the curtains starched, the windows all undimmed,
and you must save the eggplant from decline
in a salvaged plastic bucket, red, mud-trimmed,

because you cannot stand to see it fade
and lose its half-formed fruit, what do we owe
those forty-year-old marriage vows we made,
but laughter at the life-long fights we know

will plague us until one goes to the grave
and, like this sonnet, will not be resolved?

Feeding the Birds

I watch you fill the feeders — raveled threads
hanging from your out-at-elbows coat —
birds, squirrels, raccoons, the lame stray cat,
you brave the wind and rain to see them fed.

Hands dripping suds, I watch you, head and nape
swaddled in your shapeless black sock cap —
its weave a snarl of lathe shavings, chisel chips.
Coat and cap, your wing bars, your crown stripes.

When our wide-mawed nestlings squawked for nurture
I fancied I was caged by need. I fought —
a swift come down the flue and caught —
flinging against this window toward free air.

No cage, of course, but my own hungering
to stay, though I starved in the staying.

For My Valentine,
a Modern Pastural With a Lot of Bull

You always remember, I forget,
some funny card, a supermarket bag
of candy bars — another small regret,
another prick of conscience that will nag

until distracted I forget again.
You keep our calendar, can put a number
on the summer a searing west wind brought no rain,
the winter a blizzard caused our cows to wander.

Wooly-Bully would have followed his herd
into that trailer, had his nose inside,
when that hotshot hit him with a prod.
Ineluctable ton of wounded pride,

he turned and faded, black into a black
and white midnight. Last seen headed east
between the drifts, along the single track
of cleared highway. He went home. In the peace

of dawn we found him docile at the barn.
He liked his sweet feed. And so do I.
Which is why I've spun this cocked-up yarn
about a bull. I've no more sense of time

than he and I'm bull-headed but I know
where to find my green pastures. In lieu
of all the sweet remembrances I owe
I offer you these lines. Valentine: be mine.

Ephemera

I crash through,
find a grove,
sycamore, ash,
a single maple.

The deer take refuge here
unhampered by what excludes me —
blackberry canes,
goldenrod,
swarms of viceroys
and bees.

Along the leaf-mold floor,
a twisting grapevine
binds all into slow silence.

Forty years since the astonished dog
cornered a crawdad in this spot
beside a bale of hay.
Forty years since we gave up farming
this wet-weather streambed,
pocked by limestone caverns,
unfit to mow or plow.

Focused on the nearer quick —
children, garden, livestock —
I did not see this wilderness
of vines and saplings
transform into a woods.

What seems still is moving.

Our house moves westward
half an inch a year.

Homeplace with Birds and Trees

The old black locusts that line the driveway drop
a few more limbs with every storm but honey the air
with bloom each spring — a bloom that covers the yard
like snow when the oriole's an orange flicker
between sycamore and oak. The mourning doves
call out from the cedar every summer dusk and dawn.
The moon rises behind the sugar maple, June's sun
sets behind the ash, December's behind the sweet gum.
These periods of home I know as my tongue knows the map
of my teeth, but in the bite of winter's wind, I've been
on speaking terms with the serpent, scorned songbirds,
thought to try my wing beside the red-tailed hawk,
to haunt the owl's desaturated light. My hold
is the catbird's aria, the chickadee's bobbing flight,
the rhythm of your step when you come in from the shop.

Jaws of Life

A beast lurks, a trap mouth gapes
and sounds no warning tuba
glide from E to F.

In the unwary confidence
of a housewifely mood,
I sit cross-legged on the floor,
sort jeans — for the Good Will,
for the trash, for the mending basket.

Bottom of the box, last pair,
both legs slit, ankle to waist.

Saw-toothed jaw
of a great white shark,
hydraulic forceps wrench
babes from the belly
of a smashed Geo Prism

I was too late to see the firemen drag
our sons out of the wreckage,
the paramedic slice the denim.
You saw it all
in the pulsing lights of rescue trucks
that slashed a country night.

You didn't talk about it.
I didn't ask.
We lived speechless
days in waiting rooms,
faked sleep in hospital recliners

A spring-loaded steel trap
from the back of the closet:
Here is blood,
here, scattered burns
from the exploded battery.

Bonfire

After the fire has died I lie tangled
in the sheets with you, bake my aches
against the hot brick of your back.
Ambition dwindles
in the drowsy flow of your breath.

What need of belief to relieve
the black and white of winter,
the shudder of flesh like a branch
after the bird has flown. Coals blink,
then turn cold ash.

Residency

When I say this bed is way too soft,
I mean it's way too empty. Nearly a week
I've slept in it and scarcely rumpled the sheets.
I miss a certain heat, a restless tossing.

When I say this cabin's way too still,
I mean no one's breathing here but me,
no footsteps on the floorboards, no spring-creak
from another chair. I talk to the gray squirrel.

This place has mountain water, mountain air,
tremendous oaks and poplars in the woods,
three meals a day, and the dictionary's
unabridged, if old. I'm cared for, care-
less as a child, and the work I've done is good.
I'd be a fool to leave, but the heart's contrary.

An Old Lover's Invitation
to Practice a Different Alchemy

Adept of the chisel, the carbide burr,
if you should recant, if you are inclined
to renounce your transmuting grind,
we could mind our garden, plough a furrow.

Let us pick line items for our agenda
of solace, revise winter's grim prospectus
with resurgence upward thrusting as asparagus,
abandon ourselves, abundant as floribunda.

You shape your substance in a shop that's strewn
with wood chips made by shaves and scraping planes,
you smooth what goes against the grain
as you use grinding wheels to gloss your treen.

I conjure as I climb the folding stairs,
spell out rhyming runes in an attic room.
Let's try another chemistry, old groom.
We can go bare. I'll wear a flower in my hair.

II

The Woodcarver's Wife

1.
Men love blades.

Every third man's
a would-be carver.

By ones and twos
they stroll
into the market stall,
stroke the arched
cherry vessel —

curves
carved so thin
the light
shines through —

fondle the turned
pear bowl,
wood as white
as the fruit
it once produced.

I did a piece
like this once,
let me tell you
how I did it.

What tool
do you use
to get
that undercut lip?

2.
Woodcarver, my Lad with the Adze, your lips are
sculpted cherry, eyes a black locust green. Your
hair is shagbark. Gentle as falling leaves, the
touch of your fingers.

3.
Rain patters on the canopy tent.
Leaves stick like classroom cut-outs
on the skylight. Some days October
is bright and blue as advertised,
but on craft fair weekends, the month
is apt to show its drizzly side.

Carved wood no longer welcomes rain.

We let the side flaps down,
spread straw, a Walter-Raleigh cape
inviting royal tourist feet.

4.
Woodcarver, my Knave with a Shave, beguile with
long-bent gouges, dazzle with diamond-honed chisels.
Join me. We'll be mortise and tenon, dovetails,
butterfly wedges.

5.
Chain saws
pole saws
bow saws
adzes
scoops
scorps
mauls
wedges

Heart wood
sap wood
straight grain
curves
knots
spaltings
fiddleback
burls

Band saws
scroll saws
crosscuts, rips
and jigs

Chisels
gouges
lathes
and planes
as many and golden
as autumn leaves:
fingers and fores
jointers and jacks
rabbets and scrubs

6.
Woodcarver, my Swain with the Plane, you shed your
shavings everywhere, in the wash, the bathroom
sink. Your art's seductive but chips between the
sheets don't entice me.

7.
It's October so we have spoon blanks
in the microwave — carved green,
ready to be dried in this kiln —
sanded spoons on the oven rack,

the whistler on the tea kettle dismantled
and, by means of aluminum foil and a clamp,
made into a steamer to raise the grain.

Stacks of Rubbermaid tubs filled with stock
serve as coffee tables, ottomans.

We eat pizza and cold sandwiches on paper plates,
only the cats feed on a regular schedule.

8.
Woodcarver, my Scamp with a Scorp, our union
cups us deep in heartwood that, polished dark by
use, resists decay, thus outlasting younger
juicier sapwood.

9.
Rock maple, water
maple, sugar maple,
black cherry, black
walnut, black locust,
black oak, burr oak,
hickory, ash, poplar,
sycamore, sweet gum,
beech, pawpaw,
hackberry, mulberry,
dogwood, redbud,
even the invasive honeysuckle
that spreads by roots
and grows in gnarled profusion,
that in its age makes
a canopy to shelter deer,

trees grow where they will
on this place
unless ice breaks
or wind uproots.

III

Fulcrum

For my heart I walked
the ridge, as though aimed
at the bull's-eye moon
on the horizon.
At the fence, I turned —
a fiery sun skimmed
sycamores. I raised
my right hand as if
to touch the moon, my
left toward the sun.
That's when I saw her,
under the burr oak,
a doe, still as stone,
her round eye looking
at me, poised to run.

On the Eve of Leap Day

Owls talk to night.
And the moon,
first quarter,
dims Orion.

Bloom —
fanfaring daffodil —
is grayed
by this reflective light,
is betrayed —
out of its time,
extraordinary —
by balmy promise
in February,
and the false shelter
of the house.

Tomorrow,
hard realism,
frost,
and sorrow.

This night, the owls
celebrate
good hunting,
calling mate to mate —
to start the mouse
for a nuptial feast —
and two eggs
on a stolen nest.

First Day of Spring

This first day when light outlasts the dark
we dine on kale that stood the winter freeze.
Although the ground is mud and trees are stark,

this mustard feasts, first, our eyes — early leaves
crinkling purple-edged in the weak sun —
and then our tongues. We are shameless thieves,

cutpurses of growth barely begun,
such is our need, our greed for succulence.
The winter has been gray and long.

In Kroger's bins, well-traveled ranks of greens
rival cardboard, only the stuff in cans
is worse, bordering on obscene.

I wash these tiny leaves my palm can span
while olive oil heats in the frying pan.

Playing Chicken

Chevrons flashing,
a mockingbird
flits from pumphouse
door, left open,
to cistern top,
from cistern to
a mulberry
sapling we failed
to cut last fall.
He plans a raid
on the tabby
we call Miss White
for her stockings
and snowy breast.
She comes and goes.
We feed her when
she's here, kibble
the mockingbird
has eyes to steal.
We watch them through
a rainspeckled
windshield. We have
schedules to keep
in bad weather.
No use shooing
the bird. The cat,
who seems focused
on her bowl, would
rather eat fowl,
and she is quick.
You turn the key.
We drive away.

Poem Beginning With a Line From Helen Losse

Even the storm invites our trust,
the wind that rends, the bolt that jolts us
from visions of resurrection, thrusts us,
huddling, wrapped in pelts or quilts,

down underground in basement caves
to ride out its reliable fury.
When it passes we'll clear debris —
torn trees, slashed shingles — burn and bury,

plow and plant, hope for roses
and green beans, but we know always
the slow waft, the imperceptible breezes
from that fritillary's wing is all it takes.

Memento Mori

The sky was blue, the birds sang,
daffodils swayed in the breeze,
and each blade of grass glistened.
I was planting onion sets
in earth worked fine and fragrant.
Across the fence our old Black
Angus cows grazed, the spring calves
gamboled — except for the runt.
Her sudden bawl — uncanny
gurgling bray — broke the silence.
She ran, then, frantic from cow
to cow, and after a long
minute, fell down — she was dead,
choked on her own pneumonia-
rotted lungs. That was nearly
thirty years ago, the herd
long sold, the pasture grown up
in briars and saplings, but
lately, as another spring
brings forth daffodils, I find
myself thinking of that calf,
how she butted at every
udder that looked like mother,
suckling the only source she knew —
how her need was met with kicks,
even from that which birthed her —
how the old cows seemed to know
she was no longer like them,
an eater, had already
become a feeder of grass.

Pantoum for a Late Spring

A buzzard settles on a branch beside the road,
a black hulk against a field of gray.
The space heater growls its coils red,
but the sun lends no color. Clouds hold sway.

The bird hulks black against a field of gray.
The branch shows neither leaf nor bud.
The sun lends no color. Clouds hold sway.
The season sulks and weeps, the rivers flood.

The branch shows neither leaf nor bud.
Daffodils thrust up their spears but do not bloom.
The season sulks and weeps, the rivers flood.
We might be enchanted, fallen out of time.

Daffodils thrust up their spears but do not bloom.
The space heater growls its coils red.
We might be enchanted, fallen out of time.
A buzzard settles on a branch beside the road.

Pterophylla camellifolia

A katydid prates his single-minded indictment —
She did. She did. Katy did. She did —
outside our window — all the blessed night —

But the prick for that obsessive fiddling
undoubtedly is *I wish Katy would.*
No one could call it love, that scraping bid

for genetic perpetuity, Katy wooed,
bribed like any girl on a dinner date
to accept the sperm capsule with the food.

We call it a *nuptial gift* as though this mating
were something more than blind instinct,
the goal a clutch of fertile eggs waiting

in an oak to recycle the cycle. I'm a cynic,
and I doubt it. My *winged camellia leaf*
grates coarse as a bastard file to attract

his Katy. What is it brings her, you emerald thief
of sleep, your harmony or your sound-blast?
You stand in that one tree all your life,

from July's heat to October's frost.
Stridulant but patient, you don't toss and sweat
in tangled sheets or dread your fate.

Garlic

A ghost of garlic lingers on my fingers,
the sauce is just a red stain on the plate.
I breathe the scent to feed another hunger

as one whose amorous appetite is sated
might relish a fading essence of love on the hand.
Like plague doctors, haunts in cloaks whose bated

breath was filtered from miasmic London
through hawk-beaked masks stuffed with camphor and cloves,
who shoved disease away with herb-filled wands,

I seek an anodyne odor, a savory
lest I forget the body's joys in its pains,
this clinging trace of garlic all I crave

of paradise. I want a heaven as profane
as that bone white plate, that blood-red stain.

Toxicodendron radicans

In August, wearing long sleeves and latex
gloves, I tug a three-leafed whorl, coy
among the spear-like iris. Vine and rhizome
both were here long before I came.

Each year I fight the poison ivy to a draw.
My aunt says I should start over, plow up
this bed of daffodils and iris. But heirlooms
grow here. I claw the earth with condomed

fingers, grasp the root and heave
at occult tendrils tough and entwined
as my Southern Baptist heritage.
It creeps for yards at grass roots,

and I am pulled along its path, a fisher
hooked into Leviathan. Leaves, grasses,
mulch fly like water from that taut line,
until it breaks, and the creature sounds.

Hummingbirds

Late summer hummingbirds
flock to the phlox and hollyhocks
the rose of sharon by the fence.

The hummingbird is a bird absurd,
a speed that shocks, a form that mocks
gravity and common sense.

Tobacco Barn

A wake of turkey vultures makes a roost
of its ruined roof, perches on its poplar rafters
forty feet above the ground. They swoop
in low over the yard, six feet of raptor

wing, their shadows gliding over the grass.
Those four-by-fours that stood a century or more,
oak pegs locking tenon into mortise,
have gone beyond our power to restore.

Gone, too, those broganed acrobats who scaled
the tiers to stand, legs spread from rail to rail,
who'd bend and lift four feet of split hickory
stick strung with stalks of sap-heavy burley.

One above the other, these men made
a vertical bucket brigade, raising the burley
from under their feet and hoisting it over their heads
until the crop was hung from packed-dirt floor

to top plate in all the five bents. Did our barn
stand when our grandmothers woke to the midnight beat
of hooves? When they reached to touch their husbands, warm
beside them? Or to find the cold of empty sheets?

When hooded men rode out, they burned the crops
of farmers who refused to join the Equity, those Night
Riders, union zealots who meant to stop
Duke's trust. When tobacco money spurred that fight,

these barns bore the load of an economy.
The shell of ours will stand a few years more
the uneasy tenancy of this scavenger colony —
but vultures are magnificent when they soar.

August Tomatoes

The pewee cries his name again and again
to begin this August Sunday. I tongue my gums.
I've gorged on Big Boys, Black Russians, plums
until my mouth is sore, and still the garden

ripens more. Is that pewee bent
on one last reproductive fling? Why sing
so wistfully when other birds refrain?
Pewee must see that summer's light is spent —

must feel the change — a stillness in the air —
even as tomatoes grow like Jack's
beanstalk — so big we'll cut them with an ax.
Pewee, it's the fattening time of year.

Stop pining. Accept my invitation to dine
on flea beetles infesting our tomato vines.

End of Summer

Bluster and blue sky,
gust-driven locust
leaves chiseled from the sun,
an oak lit neon green,
its limbs that sway in
their dance with the wind,
my arthritic hip,
its ache as I skip
and limp in the cold.

ID_END_U20# IV

Doxology

Perched in the ash, topmost twig,
the oriole, orange as a sweat-drop fallen

from the sun, sings praise for his giant twin,
blazing on the horizon.

His cooler cousin, the meadowlark,
bides low in the fence-row brush, saves

his yellow praise for the risen star.
Oriole, sun, and meadowlark

from whom all blessings flow:
what is this human urge

to slaughter deity?
Who will summon the day

when these small gods are gone?

Duet

    An epithalamium for Thomas on his 60th birthday

I can no longer sleep on my back,
I wake myself snoring. This morning
I woke to our duet, gentle buzzing
a little out of time. We've come to this:
unmelodious, pot-bellied, stiff. We start
each day with variations on a theme of ache.

We sanctified our joining with a session.
My Dad-Dad said if that boy gets hold of
a guitar, there won't be no wedding, but he
was the one who played his mail-order mandolin
till midnight passed, sipping the Chianti he called
good sour wine. You and Johnny B and Jeff
played as his side men. Johnny still plays a lick
he learned from my grandfather that night.
We ate home-made cake, smoked Marlboros.
Daddy traded jig steps with Sally, slugged his
Heaven Hill from a brown paper bag.

Side by side, Daddy and Dad-Dad sleep
in a country churchyard, and Pat —
who helped me bake those cakes,
whose parlor table served us as an altar,
who stood by my side when we made our pledge —
died in the fall of lung cancer. This January
dawn I compose myself in the warmth
of you along my length, grateful you're
still my side man in this sometimes off-
key, always modulating measure.

After 40 Years

The towering black locust that stands south of the house
is infested with mistletoe now, two clumps in the highest bough.
The parasite attached too late to bless us with its essence:
to hold us safe from lightning. The bolt that crippled
the ash twenty years ago has left it hollow at the center,
a stairwell for squirrels. They whirligig around its trunk
these April days, a chase that might be love
or war. Hard in a long marriage to discern Ares
from Eros. Though lately we say our prayers to Anteros,
that mirror twin of passion, compassion, with butterfly wings.
So where once you stood at the threshold and sang
Raise high the roofbeam, your member vertical as a drill,
mine in answer deep and fiery as a hearth,
today we huddle by the dwindling embers and remember.

Hearth Goddess

Attired in black and framed in silver paint —
scroll work topped by coronet, the glass
domed as a watch crystal and just as quaint —

the woman sits upright. A light rouge blushes
her cheeks, rose softens her tight lips.
She wears a maiden aunt's colors, nothing so crass

as red. Left hand hidden by the Bible in her lap,
her right dangles at the wrist. Right hand
and face the only flesh she shows, ear lobes

and fingers without jewels, expression bland,
unsmiling as befits the solemn portrait,
seated on a mirrored hallway stand —

she might wait for a groom who'll bring the gaited
mare, sidesaddled, curb-bitted, around to the mounting
block. Her brow is arched, her nose is straight,

her eyes a forthright brown. She shows no jowls
though her upswept hair is iron gray.
How proper. But when we moved into the house,

we found her in the attic, secreted way
under the eaves, as though she had been banished,
but was kin too close to cast away.

We brought her downstairs, hung her over the piano,
our Hestia, our Brighid, our household muse.
Does she like her role as guardian ancestor?

I search her face sometimes, looking for cues
but that which she knows, she knows how to refuse.

Clothes Make the Man

If I could count how many times I've nagged
at you to throw those ratty things away —
the tattered coat too worn to call a rag,
the cap a trap for wood chips, sawdust, shavings,

the threadbare jeans, the duct-tape-patched galoshes.
Good enough for work, you say, as if work
were worth no more than shreds and iron-on patches,
as if castoffs might risk a witch's curse

like snips of fingernail and hair. If I
could sum my wardrobe grievances, what then?
Would it be *sartor resartus*? husband transformed?
After all these years I wonder why
I care. I wouldn't want a Dapper Dan,
though a certain tidiness might work a charm.

What Bugs Us

Termites eat away the window frames,
spiders web between the blind and screen,
a variety of insects for which I have no name
swarm my reading light and die in obscene

numbers. Crickets sing behind the walls,
wasps build major colonies in the eaves,
ants in the pantry, moths in the cornmeal,
flies in the attic, in the rafters, wood bees.

We are slow, my love, and dissolution
in this buggy world is quick. Every-
thing that is not eating is being eaten,
even, it seems, our house. They say the solution
is industry, but what if it were reverie?
The end's the same: we eat until we're eaten.

Attrition

It's too late now to whine about the state
of things. Of course the kitchen tap will leak
if you don't replace the washers. Time will grate
on matter like a rat-tail rasp. The state
of things isn't steady. The drip in the attic won't wait
until you turn the last page of *War and Peace*.
Next week's too late. Don't whine about the state
of things. Of course the kitchen tap still leaks.

Wasted

> *when we hot-rodded over God's front lawn,*
> *and Death kept blinking*
> —Tony Hoagland

I'd like to say I sacrificed my spine
to too much smoking anything on offer,
too much drinking fine or rotgut booze,
too much screwing too many beautiful blonds.
I may already be an old woman
but not because too many up-to-eleven
rock bands shook my bones until they crumbled
like the walls of Jericho. The one woman
I know who lived that life is seventy-five
this year, moves like a model, out-drinks
men twenty years her junior. I rammed
no hot rod, metaphorical or real,
onto God's front lawn. I was the mouse
crouching under a desk in a hard-to-find hole
in His fluorescent-lighted basement,
where I sniffed for crumbs of pension
and insurance. Death didn't blink for me
because I made no challenge. Instead,
like Eve, I hid and hoped he'd pass me by.

Dissonance

Apparitions rise in their shrouds.

Pulling the covers to my chin,
I stretch and test my joints against the cold,
gaze from my dark into the bright night.
The Hunger Moon makes shadows on the snow,
a landscape
alien as an owl's eyes.
She is out there somewhere,
nested in the hollow of an oak,
brooding a single egg.

That revenant lurch
stalks my waking.
What if I board my windows,
buy sturdy shoes,
watch for rough spots in the sidewalk?

I listen for the fluting owl,
hear only the rasp of my own breath.

Diagnosis

after a line from William Stafford

If it should happen you wake up
the dragon, feel upon your nape
the flutter of its breath as you leap
and run — don't think you will escape —
the beast has wings, it will catch up.

A Fairytale

Yes, I wore the white satin dress
that fell shoulder to ankle,
a cloth caress a sudden elegance,

but the hem was stained with red
wine I'd spilled and so
were the soles of my bare feet.

Once the bottle held a cheap merlot,
but now it bears no stain of liquor,
no sign of label. It's washed

ashore, free of sin, though someone tried
to seal the cork with red candle drippings.
The wax peeled and set the genie free.

Helmet-headed, lead-footed as a deep-
sea diver, it lurches through the labyrinth
where I wander without a ball of string.

The thing has no need to solve the puzzle.
It's as unrelenting as the Tortoise. Am I
Bugs Bunny in a sprint to the wrong turn?

Those three wishes are always a trick.
Cinderella may escape the ashes
but first she is required to dance on glass.

Aubade

Somewhere down the road a farm dog barks.
I don't hear them much these days, even
in the country. Nor will I hear a lark
at sunrise, only mourning doves and robins.
I've given up on sleep again, content
in the company of crickets and phantoms.
I can't say I find much to lament
about the end of one more night. After
forty years, romance is mostly spent,
its cause better served by craft
than Cupid's pricks, the poet's art.
The sun pinks the eastern sky, as soft
as heat recalled, In our cedar's dark heart,
the doves murmur. A pickup growls
along the road, the dog is still. The threat
may have been coydogs that yowl
just beyond our leaning barn.
Their frenzy sends me on the prowl,
securing locks in every room.
I'd forfeit passion for that ray of sun
that streaks the grass. The dawn has come.

Medjool Dates

I eat them from a bowl, lick
their succulence from my thumb and finger,
tongue the whorls and pads, suck
my own sweet flesh, linger

in the feedback loop of warm and wet.
You sit across the table, chew the ball
of your thumb as we talk, incising small
pain, a twinge to let you forget

an ache. We speak of extremities, ends,
of fingers that crook, yet will not bend
to our will, of years that we can number
on our fingers and our thumbs.

Dry October

The ground is hard with drought. The shovel
cannot bite. The posthole digger bounces,
rattles the dried-out leaves. A foot down, the soil
is gray. We find no forgiving softness.

We bury the cat shallow, cover the grave
with planks, weight them with a rusty cylinder head.
The sun's last rose fades west. The moon
is humpbacked. We crunch back to the house.

Numerology

> *the dried-up riverbeds*
> *of ancient mothers*
> — Rilke

I'm brittle as a stick of stale Juicy Fruit,
porous to the bone; the specialist lays
three fingers on my knee and says, in solemn
Syrian accent, *You must not fall.* Eve fell.
But not in Syria. More likely over the border
in Iraq, between those rivers where the flow
has not dried up, not of water nor of blood,
and not of oil rendered from ancient bones.
Somewhere I've read that dinosaurs were good
mothers. Thirty-four years ago today,
eight days after I'd turned thirty-four,
I birthed twin sons. Today, on his birthday,
my younger e-mails photos of his own
five-day-old twins, swaddled and capped
like cocooned caterpillars about to emerge —
as what? Giant luna moths? Grandchildren?
What do all these numbers mean?
On the Fourth of July, nineteen-seventy-four,
a drunken graduate student named Stan studied
my palm, foresaw one pregnancy and a long life.
His first prediction came to pass, but with a twist.
His second twists me too soon into a crone,
my sexuality, my very smell gone strange.
Milton says God set the celestial clock in motion
when Eve took the serpent's bait and bit.
Death and Time the twins born of that fall.

Stitches Out of Time

I feed the flimsy yarn through my fingers,
a thread soft as the infant who'll wear
this vest. It takes slow form,
a single thread drawn loop
through loop in a running knot.
Newborn to creeper, the baby grows faster.
More efficient, then, and certainly cheaper,
to buy a cute, colorful, fire-retardant shirt
from a big box store. And I will.
But I want this meditative task,
to linger over every row.
The babe doesn't care.
She has vital work to do.
A grandmother doesn't count right now,
except these stitches from an older time.

Christmas Day, 2010

Look, you cried and I saw the hawk, still
as an Audubon print, covering a scarlet spill:
the cock cardinal's tail. Saw the slope
of the kestrel's back, the wintry gold
of its eye, its half-turned head as it gazed
as if to dare my witness, hold me amazed
at carnage under our suet and sunflower seeds,
small pagan god defiant at the Christian feast.

When you flew for the camera, I glanced
away, and they were gone, killer and killed.
Just that quick we broke the spell.
The deed might not have happened, the evidence
of things seen only a shallow hole
and two red feathers lying on the snow.

Saturday Morning Cartoons

In this snap I took
the boys look
almost sad, snug
as they are, though
you show
a hint of a grin.

Three in a row
on the old green couch —
you and the twins
watched Bugs
wreak his mayhem
mesmerized
in solemn ritual.

They lounge on you,
you shelter them.

Even at five they'd learned
from you to discern
not just the artist's name
but his style,
knew a Tex Avery
from a Chuck Jones,
knew the movies from tv,
a Looney Toons
from a Merry Melody.

I can't put my finger
on a calendar square
when the ritual stopped.

Boys grow up —
blankets are spurned,
thumbs go dry —
they no longer linger
in their Pop's
embrace.

The rabbit hole,
the wrong turn at Albuquerque,
becomes a worm hole.

Luke Sky-
walker replaces
the all-American hare.

Beginning

I don't know how to begin, you say. No more
do I. How do we see begin with end
so imminent, and how do we begin
to end? There's a question mocks my store
of learning. Nor can I depend
on faith or science or the resuscitateds' stories
of white light or any other arcane lore.
We'll have no Virgil to take us by the hands.

Only one thing I know — whether or not
we're to meet on some sentimental shore —
we won't begin the ending solitary.
We spin in common orbit.
Faithful companions, like the Dog Stars,
we'll wobble our way to an end, binary.

Acknowledgements

I am grateful to the editors of the following publications in which versions of these poems appear.

Bigger than They Appear, Anthology of Very Short Poems (Accents Publishing, 2011) — "End of Summer"
Kestrel — "Christmas Day, 2010" & "What Bugs Us"
Light, A Quarterly of Light Verse — "Hummingbird"
Louisville Review — "Dry October"
NILAS Newsletter — "Toxicodendron radicans"
Now & Then: The Appalachian Magazine — "Fulcrum"
Parting Gifts — "Jaws of Life" as "A Housecleaning Day"
Passager — "Looking West"
Pegasus — "On the Eve of Leap Day"
qarrtsiluni — "Doxology"
South Carolina Review — "August Tomatoes" & "Poem beginning with a Line from Helen Losse"
Still — "An Accounting"
The Chaffin Journal — "Against Panache"
The Cortland Review — "First Day of Spring"
The Other Voices International Project — "Ephemera" as "Behind the Blackberry Thicket"
The William and Mary Review — "Medjool Dates"
Tilt-A-Whirl — "Attrition"
Umbrella — "Rough Winds" as "Sonnet 18 Revisited"
YB Poetry — "*Pterophylla camellifolia*"

"Bonfire" was originally published in my chapbook, *My Will & Testament Is on the Desk* (FootHills Publishing, 2003)
"Clearing Out" was originally published as "Trinkets" in my chapbook *Dance the Black-Eyed Girl* (Finishing Line, 2003)
"Atmospheric Conditions" was originally posted on the Accents Publishing blog as part of Lexington Poetry Month 2013

"Poem Beginning with a Line from Helen Losse" uses a line from
"The Danger of Pretense" from *Seriously Dangerous* (Main
Street Rag, 2011)
"Sonnenizio on a Line from Hayden Carruth" uses a line from *The
Sleeping Beauty* (Harper & Row, 1982).
"Diagnosis" uses a line from William Stafford, *Every War Has Two
Losers: William Stafford on Peace and War* (Milkweed
Editions, 2003)

Thank you to Nancy Cassell, David Cazden, Matthew Haughton, Charlie Hughes, Terry Kanago, Leatha Kendrick, Andrea O'Brien, Christina Parker, J. Stephen Rhodes, Leslie Shane, Georgia Stamper, and all of the Green River Writers, especially Ernie O'Dell, Georgia Wallace, Jean Tucker, Elaine Palencia, Harriet Leach, and Mark Brown. I am much obliged to the faculty and staff of the Carnegie Center for Literacy and Learning in Lexington, Kentucky, to Donna Long and Elizabeth Savage for believing in me, and to Judith Hower and Kathie Sauer, my crowd funders.

A special thank you to the Wildacres Retreat Center for the award of a cost-free residency in 2011. The concept and a number of the poems for this book originated there.

An extra special thank you to three of my first teachers: Verna Mae Roland, Eileen Morgan, and Jane Gentry.